W0006795

Mouse's Moon Party

by Amy Helfer

illustrated by Akemi Gutierrez

Mouse calls his friends.

"Come to my moon party!" he says.
"It will be fun!"

"I will come," Cat says.
"I will bring a cake."

Rabbit can come.
"I will bring hats,"
she says.

"I will bring milk,"
Cow says.
"A party needs milk."

"Will we dance?"
says Dog.

"Yes!" says Mouse.

It is time for the party.
Cat has the cake.
Rabbit has the hats.

Look how Cow can
pull the milk.

The moon is a
yellow ball.
See it glow?

It is a good moon
party!
We are glad we came!

Respond to Reading

Retell

Use your own words to retell details in *Mouse's Moon Party.*

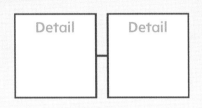

Text Evidence

1. Look at page 4. Who does Mouse call first? Key Details: Sequence

2. Look at page 8. Who comes after Cat? Key Details: Sequence

3. How do you know *Mouse's Moon Party* is a fantasy? Genre

A Mouse in the House

cage

blue jean images/Getty Images

Genre Nonfiction

Compare Texts
Read to find out about a pet mouse.

A mouse can be
a fun pet.
It is fun to watch.
It is fun to play
with a mouse.

pets

What a Pet Mouse Needs

1. a safe, clean cage
2. fresh water
3. good food
4. play time
5. love

exercise wheel

Make Connections

What things does Mouse have at his party? What does a real pet mouse need? Text to Text

15

Focus on
Science

Purpose To find out what pets need

What to Do

Step 1 Think about different kinds of pets. Choose one.

Step 2 Make a chart like this.

My pet is a _____.
My pet needs
1. _____
2. _____
3. _____

Step 3 Fill in the chart.

Conclusion Talk to a friend about what your pet needs.